100 Facts about

Dinosaurs

Copyright © 2023 By Tiki Taka.
All rights reserved. No part of the contents of this book may be reproduced or transmitted in any form or by any means without written permission from the publisher.

FACT 1

Dinosaurs have been around for more than 230 million years!

About 250 million years ago, most life on earth went extinct, and within the next ten million years or so, dinosaurs began to evolve.

The exact timing of when dinosaurs first entered the scene is up for question, but we know for sure that it was between 230-245 million years ago.

FACT 2

Dinosaurs lived during the Mesozoic era.

The Mesozoic era roughly ran from 245 to 66 million years ago and is generally divided into three time periods: the Triassic, Jurassic, and Cretaceous periods.

Dinosaurs first evolved during the Triassic period, increased in number and variety in the Jurassic period, evolved even further during the Cretaceous period, and then, well, pretty much just died off really.

FACT 3

They evolved from reptiles the size of house cats.

From around 244 to 242 million years ago, small yet agile reptiles known as dinosauromorphs rapidly increased and spread across the world.

While they were far too small to come even close to the top of the food chain, they were speedy enough to escape predators for long enough to evolve into dinosaurs!

FACT 4

Dinosaurs are still alive and with us today!

Don't go running and screaming for help, though, unless you happen to be deathly afraid of chickens!

In fact, all birds are descendants of dinosaurs — even the humble hummingbird.

All the non-avian dinosaurs went extinct, but the avian dinosaurs evolved over the millennia into birds.

FACT 5

Pterodactyls are not actually dinosaurs.

Pterodactyls, along with all other winged dinosaur-like reptiles, belong not to the dinosaur family but are classified as Pterosaurs.

While Pterosaurs are indeed related to dinosaurs, the connection is quite distant, splitting off from the archosaurs.

FACT 6

Dinosaurs are split into two main categories.

To put it simply, either a dinosaur is a saurischian (Greek for "lizard-hipped"), or they're an ornithischian (Greek for "bird-hipped").

Funnily enough, the lizard-hipped dinosaurs are more commonly related to modern-day birds, while the bird-hipped dinosaurs all went extinct!

FACT 7

The first dinosaur was named before we even knew dinosaurs existed.

In 1815 William Buckland, a geology professor from Oxford University, came across the skeleton of an animal unlike any previously recorded.

Deciding that it was some long-extinct form of reptile, he named it "Megalosaurus" (Greek for "great lizard").

FACT 8

Dinosaurs were only classified in 1842.

Just seven years after Buckland discovered the megalosaurus, a geologist and his wife came upon a new iguana-like skeleton in Sussex, England, which they named "Iguanadon."

More fossils started turning up, so Sir Richard Owen (who later founded London's Natural History Museum) classified the fossils as belonging to the "Dinosauria" family (Greek for "terrible lizards").

FACT 9

Dinosaurs weren't named as such because they inspired terror.

When Sir Richard Owen came up with the name for dinosaurs, he meant the word terrible in a different sense.

He described them as being "fearfully great," as in far larger in size than any previously known reptiles.

Maybe if the first fossil he came across were that of a T-Rex, he would have meant it in more of a literal sense!

FACT 10

When the iguanodon was first reconstructed, its thumb was placed on top of its nose.

It wasn't until 40 years later, in 1878, when more iguanodon skeletons were unearthed, that we realized the long, spiky thumb was not like a rhino's horn but an odd thumb-like digit!

To this day, paleontologists still haven't come up with a good reason why iguanodons developed such long spiky thumbs, although it may have been for self-defense.

FACT 11

The megalosaurus was so popular in the 19th century that Charles Dickens included it in one of his novels.

In the opening lines of Charles Dickens's Bleak House, the famous British author imagines what it would be like to come across a megalosaurus waddling through the streets of London.

Amazingly enough, considering the size and likely ferocity of the megalosaurus, Dickens didn't paint the megalosaurus in a fearsome light – describing it instead as an "elephantine lizard."

FACT 12

You can tell the difference between a dinosaur fossil and a stone by licking it.

While this doesn't sound like the most legitimate approach, paleontologists may find themselves doing this on a daily basis!

If you lick a suspected fossil, it will stick ever so slightly to your tongue because fossils are more porous than stones.

FACT 13

More than 900 different dinosaurs roamed Earth.

From this point onward, when we say dinosaur, assume we're talking about non-avian dinosaurs – as there are also plenty of birds out there today still!

The 900 or so dinosaurs we're talking about here are those which have been deemed valid, as in there are enough fossilized remains to assure us that they are genuine dinosaur species.

There are actually plenty more potential species, many already with names, that are non-valid due to a lack of solid evidence!

FACT 14

Dinosaurs lived on all of Earth's continents.

When dinosaurs first came onto the scene in the Triassic period, some 230 million years ago, the Earth's continents were clustered together into one giant supercontinent called Pangaea.

Over the following 165 million years that dinosaurs roamed the earth, Pangaea slowly drifted apart, separating many dinosaur species from each other.

FACT 15

The largest dinosaurs were the titanosaurs.

The titanosaurs were a subspecies of sauropods, herbivorous four-legged leviathans with long necks and small heads.

They stomped around quite late in the dinosaur age, from about 145-66 million years ago.

It's quite debatable which of them is the largest due to poorly preserved fossils, but the argentinosaurus is the best bet, measuring in at 99 to 110 tons (90 to 100 tonnes)!

FACT 16

The smallest sauropod was only slightly heavier than a bull.

The europasaurus was a pretty remarkable sauropod; it appeared like one in all respects but never grew to anything like the monumental sizes of its cousins.

While its 19' 8" (6 meters) length is still quite long, it's nothing like its football-pitch-sized relatives!

FACT 17

Gallimimuses had beaks instead of teeth.

This odd-looking theropod once roamed around during the late Cretaceous period in what is now Mongolia.

Although its name translates to "chicken mimic," it actually more closely resembled a giant ostrich with arms.

FACT 18

Most of the world's dinosaur fossils are found in three places.

The high-altitude badlands of China, Argentina, and North America hold some of the largest amounts of fossils, or at least easily accessible ones anyway.

The reality is that much of the world is covered in fossils, but they're easily unearthed in desert-like environments due to the lack of vegetation!

FACT 19

Some pterosaurs were covered in fur.

I don't know about you, but that doesn't make them seem any less scary.

They would have appeared similar in many ways to a fruit bat, but at a much, much larger scale!

FACT 20

Most fossilized dinosaur bones aren't actually bones anymore.

The fossilization process most commonly happens when something gets trapped between layers of sediment or sand and remains there for millions of years.

These remains then get surrounded by a layer of water, which replaces the original organic material with various minerals, creating a rock-like copy!

FACT 21

Some dinosaurs were covered in feathers!

Until the 1990s, it was believed that all dinosaurs were covered in large scales, much like today's reptiles.

Since then, more evidence emerged that the group of dinosaurs, known as theropods, was covered in feathers.

Theropods include velociraptors, tyrannosaurus rexes, and the ancestors of today's birds.

FACT 22

Most dinosaurs weren't very brainy.

While they may have been mighty fearsome beasties, dinosaurs would have been incredibly easy to outwit due to their pea-sized brains.

For example, the stegosaurus had a brain the size of a lime in a body up to 29 feet and 6 inches (9 meters) long.

FACT 23

Two of the world's most famous paleontologists hated each other.

In the late 19th century, there was little interest in paleontology in North America, something which Othniel Charles Marsh and Edward Drinker Cope sought to change.

While they began as friends, they soon turned on each other in a life-long competition to prove who was the greater scientist.

While both men ultimately degraded themselves and could be said to have both lost, they essentially birthed the entire US paleontology scene in the process.

FACT 24

The smartest dinosaurs were all carnivores.

Specifically, the predatory theropods were the ones to watch out for in prehistoric times.

At the lower end of this group, the infamous t-rex had a significantly larger brain than the herbivorous stegosaurus.

The smartest of all were the small, agile theropods like the velociraptor or the troodontids, which had similar brains to today's flightless birds.

FACT 25

The nigersaurus replaced its teeth as often as every fourteen days!

This remarkable sauropod had rows and rows of teeth in reserve, hidden away in its mouth.

When a set of teeth wore out, they would fall out, and the next row would move into position.

FACT 26

If it lives in water, it isn't a dinosaur.

Some of the first fossils of ancient reptiles found were great beastly creatures that, by all appearances, predominately lived underwater and were promptly classified as plesiosaurs.

While they also share a common ancestor with dinosaurs, they're so distantly related that they remain in their own group.

FACT 27

The dinosaur with the longest name was the micropachycephalosaurus.

Try saying that all in one go without stopping!

With 23 letters and nine syllables, the micropachycephalosaurus has an incredibly difficult and long name for such a small dinosaur.

Its name, after all, translates to "small thick-headed lizard."

FACT 28

We don't actually know what killed the dinosaurs, and we may never find out.

The Cretaceous extinction was one of the largest mass extinctions the world has ever seen, but as it happened some 66 million years ago, we may never be able to tell how it happened. Instead, all we have are theories.

Around this time, an asteroid crashed into Earth just off the coast of Mexico, which started a chain of events that led to the extinction of all non-avian dinosaurs.

While it's a good theory, and is the most commonly accepted one, there are also many other ideas for how the dinosaurs died out — with climate change being the other most likely culprit!

FACT 29

All four-legged dinosaurs were herbivores.

That's not to say that all herbivorous dinosaurs were four-legged, though.

While that is a common misconception, it turns out that there were quite a few herbivorous dinosaurs that could walk on two legs, at least for short periods of time!

FACT 30

Dinosaurs didn't all go extinct at the same time, either.

The asteroid which crashed into Earth didn't wipe out all the dinosaurs at once.

Instead, it likely triggered a chain reaction of events that completely changed the face of the planet.

This, of course, didn't happen overnight, but over the following few hundred or even thousands of years, slowly killing off all but the avian dinosaurs.

FACT 31

In the entirety of the first Jurassic Park movie, there were just 15 minutes in which dinosaurs were shown.

Nine minutes of those were taken up by animatronic dinosaurs, such as the large robotic T-Rex.

The other nine were all CGI – an impressive feat for a film released in 1993!

FACT 32

Some dinosaurs had four wings.

Adorably named the Microraptor, this minuscule bird-like dinosaur measured just 2-3 feet (60-90 cm) long and weighed about 2-3 pounds (1-1.36 kg).

There have been hundreds of fossilized remains uncovered since the turn of the 21st century, and all fossils clearly show that Microraptors had wings on both its front and rear legs!

FACT 33

Corythosauruses used their crests to make loud, trombone-like sounds.

Their crests were hollow in many parts and were directly connected to their nasal passages.

When the corythosaurus exhaled, the noise they produced would have been quite loud but also low-frequency.

FACT 34

The majority of dinosaurs were herbivores.

The carnivorous dinosaurs were apex predators that lived at the top of the food chain.

As they lived at the top, there were much fewer of them than other dinosaurs.

There would have been vast herds of herbivorous dinosaurs of varying sizes roaming the Earth, which were then hunted by much smaller packs of predators.

FACT 35

A new triceratops relative was nicknamed "Hellboy," after the popular comic book character.

Officially named Regaliceratops peterhewsi, after the geologist who first discovered it, this fossil soon gained its comical nickname due to its unique skull shape.

While it appeared much like a triceratops, it sported small horns just above each eye, much like Hellboy.

FACT 36

Some carnivorous dinosaurs had hollow bones.

Like today's birds, dinosaurs such as velociraptors and T-rexes actually stored air in their bones to improve their breathing abilities.

This difference essentially made these dinosaurs lighter on their feet and allowed them to breathe much more efficiently – everything a predator would need!

FACT 37

When King Edward VII saw sketches of the first diplodocus skeleton, he requested a cast of it for London's Natural History Museum.

King Edward VII first came across the sketch while visiting the home of a prominent Scottish businessman in 1902.

The plaster-cast diplodocus replica soon gained the nickname "dippy" and was a central feature of the museum for over a century!

FACT 38

Diplodocuses had the longest tails of any known dinosaurs.

While it wasn't the longest dinosaur ever, the diplodocus was certainly well endowed with its tail, which measured an incredible 46 feet (14 m) long!

FACT 39

The plates that Stegosauruses had along their backs weren't used for defense.

This was the most commonly held theory for a long time but has since been replaced with two main possibilities – the plates were either used as a display for other stegosauruses or even to help regulate their temperature!

These plates were chock-full of blood vessels, so they may have pumped warm blood to them, which then cooled on the large, flat surfaces – much like a car's radiator!

FACT 40

The average dinosaur weighed about 7,700 lbs (3,493 kg).

That's the mathematical average when you compare the weight of all known dinosaurs, that is.

And how big was the average dinosaur, you ask?

Still quite large – somewhere between an elephant and a rhino.

FACT 41

There's a fossil of a protoceratops and a velociraptor caught in the middle of a deathmatch.

The pair were in the middle of an intense battle when they were trapped under a landslide, locking them in place for millions of years.

The protoceratops may have been on the losing foot, as the velociraptor had sunk its long claws deep into its neck, but it wasn't a one-sided battle.

The velociraptor was also fighting for its life, as the protoceratops had locked its jaws onto its right arm, and broken it.

FACT 42

Some dinosaurs may have shed their skins.

From the evidence we have so far, it doesn't look like they shed their skins all in one go like modern snakes or lizards.

In fact, the only evidence we have is from bird-like dinosaurs, who shed small chunks of skin from between their feathers.

FACT 43

The oviraptor had a beak instead of teeth.

Fossils of this funny-looking theropod were unearthed in Mongolia and dated back about 85-75 million years ago.

It wasn't the only dinosaur with a beak, though, but part of a larger family of beaked dinosaurs called Oviraptoridae. Because it had no teeth, it was originally believed to eat eggs, hence its name – "egg thief."

It's since been theorized that oviraptors were omnivorous.

FACT 44

People debated whether the brontosaurus was a unique species for more than a hundred years.

In 1879 the first brontosaurus skeleton was unearthed.

Due to its similarity to the already discovered apatosaurus, many doubted whether it truly was a new species.

As such, all brontosaurus skeletons were marked as apatosauruses.

This continued until 2015, when an in-depth study into the relationships between these species confirmed that the brontosaurus was indeed its own species, and so the name was reclaimed.

FACT 45

The dinosaur with the longest claws was the therizinosaurs.

Quite rightly named the "reaping lizard," this horrifying dinosaur had three long 3.2 feet (1 m) scythe-like claws on each arm.

With claws that long, it's also the longest clawed animal to have ever existed!

FACT 46

Dinosaurs were distantly related to crocodiles.

Crocodiles, pterosaurs, mosasaurs, ichthyosaurs, and dinosaurs all have a few things in common.

They're all reptiles, to start with, but it's more than that.

They all evolved from one common group of ancestors, the archosaurs, between 250 to 200 million years ago.

FACT 47

Some dinosaurs intentionally swallowed huge stones.

These stones, known as gastroliths, may have helped herbivores to grind down the vegetation they ate into more digestible pieces.

Plesiosaurs also may have swallowed stones to help manage their buoyancy, much like tadpoles and axolotl do today.

FACT 48

Up until 1923, we didn't know how dinosaurs were born.

We suspected that dinosaurs laid eggs, as they were reptiles after all, but there hadn't been any proof.

The smoking gun came in 1923 when a collection of fossilized dinosaur eggs were discovered in Mongolia.

FACT 49

Not all dinosaurs laid the same kinds of eggs.

Nearly all fossilized dinosaur eggs that have been discovered had hard shells, much like bird's eggs today.

A few fossilized soft-shelled eggs were unearthed that date back to the first dinosaurs, suggesting that the earliest dinosaurs laid their eggs and buried them like modern lizards.

FACT 50

Some ichthyosaurs gave birth to their infants tail-first, to prevent them from drowning before they reached the water's surface.

Although they were reptiles, ichthyosaurs such as the Stenopterygius were similar in many ways to today's dolphins.

Instead of birthing eggs, they developed their young in embryos, only giving birth to them once they were ready to swim.

FACT 51

The longest carnivorous dinosaur was the spinosaurus.

The spinosaurus (Greek for "spine lizard") was not only the largest meat-eating dinosaur but had huge spines sticking out of its back which formed a kind of sail.

Spinosaurus fossils indicate that they could grow up to 46 feet (14 meters) long and weigh around 8 US tons (7.4 tonnes).

FACT 52

We have no idea what color dinosaurs were.

Some scientists believe that dinosaurs would have had rather dull colors, like elephants and rhinos, so they could blend in with the environment and avoid predators.

On the contrary, it's also commonly theorized that dinosaurs were actually brightly colored so that they could easily attract potential mates, much like today's birds.

In some cases, it was likely a combination of both!

FACT 53

The Quetzalcoatlus northropi had the largest wingspan out of any known pterosaurs.

Can you imagine looking into the sky and seeing a dinosaur-like creature the size of a small plane soaring overhead?

The Quetzalcoatlus northropi (named after the Mesoamerican god) lived in the late Cretaceous period and had a mind-bending 23-43 foot (7–13 m) wingspan.

FACT 54

The qantassaurus was named after Australia's main commercial airline.

This six-foot (2 m) long herbivore was first discovered during a dig in the Australian state of Victoria in 1996 but spent three years without a name.

Finally, in 1999, it was named the qantassaurus after QANTAS, the Australian airline which at the time sponsored the transport of many dinosaur fossils across Australia.

FACT 55

We're able to estimate the speed of dinosaurs from their fossilized footprints.

Unfortunately, it's incredibly challenging to figure out which footprint belonged to which dinosaur, with most tracks left unidentified.

FACT 56

One of the UK's greatest early paleontology pioneers was not recognized in her time because she was a woman.

At the beginning of the 19th century, science was still a man's line of work, making life increasingly frustrating for Mary Anning.

Despite this, she persevered and unearthed fossil after fossil, including the first-ever pterosaur found outside of Germany.

FACT 57

The fastest dinosaurs had long ostrich-like limbs.

The ostrich mimic ornithomimids were named as such because they were bird-like and covered in feathers.

From the analysis of fossilized footprints, it was ascertained that dinosaurs of this genus were among the fastest, reaching speeds up to 25 miles per hour (40 km per hour).

FACT 58

The kosmoceratops had fifteen horns sticking out of its face.

With more horns than any other known dinosaur, the kosmoceratops, a relative of the triceratops, certainly had the most ornate skull.

It lived during the late Cretaceous period, somewhere between 76-75 million years ago.

FACT 59

The velociraptors in Jurassic Park were actually a completely different raptor.

The raptors in the novel and the films were based almost entirely on deinonychuses, a completely different and much larger raptor found in the US. That said, even they weren't as large as the velociraptors in the films!

Michael Chrichton, the author of Jurassic Park, met with the discoverer of the deinonychus to learn about the raptor's behavior.

He even admitted that the raptors in his novel were deinonychuses in all but name!

FACT 60

Deinonychuses didn't use their claws to disembowel their prey.

When they were first discovered, it was believed that Deinonychus (along with many other Dromaesaurids) used their razor-sharp hind claws as a weapon.

This belief has since been questioned by many scientists, with a range of possible answers. One prominent theory is that they used their hind claws to grip onto prey so they could tear at them with their much sharper teeth.

FACT 61

Velociraptors were about the same size as turkeys.

While they were probably still pretty terrifying, they were nothing like the nightmare-inducing raptors from Jurassic Park.

In fact, more recently discovered velociraptor fossils have proved that they had long, feathered tails and wing feathers on their arms.

FACT 62

Velociraptors' name translates into "speedy thief."

Henry Fairfield Osborn, then the American Museum of Natural History president, gave the velociraptor its name in 1924.

He named it as such because of his quite accurate assessment that it would have been an incredibly swift yet agile carnivorous dinosaur.

FACT 63

The pentaceratops had the largest skull out of any known dinosaurs.

Measuring at 10.49 feet (3.2 m) high, the skull of the pentaceratops was also the largest of any animal ever to walk the earth!

FACT 64

Most dinosaurs in Jurassic Park didn't live during the Jurassic period.

While the Jurassic Park series certainly made dinosaurs much more popular, it wasn't entirely accurate.

Out of all the dinosaurs featured in the first film, only the brachiosaurus and the dilophosaurus actually belonged to the Jurassic period, while the rest mostly belonged to the Cretaceous period.

To give you an idea of how wrong this was, the Jurassic period ranged from 200 to 145 million years ago, while the Cretaceous ranged from 145 to 66 million years ago!

FACT 65

Pachycephalosaurus wyomingensis had a 9-inch (23 cm) thick skull.

This thick-headed dinosaur likely had the thickest skull of all, leading paleontologists to wonder what it could have been used for.

Some believe they would have head-butted each other to display their strength, but this theory is a little questionable as it appears their neck bones weren't strong enough to withstand such strong impacts.

FACT 66

Brachiosauruses had long, giraffe-like necks.

A herbivore like today's giraffes, the brachiosaurus made use of its long neck to feed on the choicest parts of trees that were untouched by smaller dinosaurs.

Its front legs were longer than its back legs, hence why it was given a name that translates to "arms lizard."

FACT 67

Fossilized dinosaur poop is called coprolite, and it's highly prized by collectors.

The Guinness World Record for the largest collection of coprolite is 1,277, which is owned by George Frandsen.

Frandsen first became fascinated with coprolite when he was in college, where he was studying paleontology.

His fascination comes from the fact that you're able to tell so much about a dinosaur's lifestyle and diet by examining their fossilized feces!

FACT 68

The largest piece of carnivore coprolite weighs about as much as a dachshund!

This monstrous piece of poop is also owned by George Frandsen and most likely came out of a T-Rex's rear end sometime around 70-66 million years ago.

Nicknamed "Barnum," after the man who first discovered the T-Rex, it weighs 20.47 lbs (9.28 kg) and measures 26.5 by 6.2 inches (67.5 by 15.7 cm).

FACT 69

According to Nintendo, Yoshi is not a dinosaur.

For a long time, Nintendo claimed otherwise, but now they've officially done a U-turn and stated straight up that he's not a dinosaur – he's simply a Yoshi!

FACT 70

The first complete dinosaur skeleton to be mounted in a museum was a hadrosaurus.

In 1858 William Parker Foulke discovered the first fossilized Hadrosaurus skeleton, which also happened to be the most intact dinosaur skeleton unearthed by this point.

In 1868, the hadrosaurus was mounted in the Academy of Natural Sciences in Philadelphia. It drew people from all over the world and inspired generations of future paleontologists!

FACT 71

A group of dinosaurs known as the hadrosaurs had the most teeth.

This duck-billed family of dinosaurs, which included the Edmontosaurus and Parasaurolophus, had as many as 960 flat teeth.

They used their powerful jaws and teeth to grind up plant matter into a more digestible state.

FACT 72

For 50 years, the deinocheirus was known only for its arms.

When the fossilized arms were discovered, scientists were quick to give the new dinosaur a name – deinocheirus, which translates into "terrible arms."

To be fair, going off the arms alone, this dinosaur certainly looked formidable.

When full skeletons were discovered 50 years later, this awkward-looking dinosaur became quite the laughing stock of the paleontology world!

FACT 73

Hogwarts School of Witcraft and Wizardry had its own dinosaur.

No really. In 2006, scientists decided to name a newly discovered dinosaur Dracorex hogwartsia, which translates into "dragon king of Hogwarts."

The first part of its name is inspired by the fact that this dinosaur's skull is very similar in appearance to a mythical dragon!

Unfortunately for Harry Potter fans, it turns out that the skull that the new dinosaur was based on was actually from a juvenile Pachycephalosaurus.

FACT 74

A piece of amber from Myanmar was found with a fully preserved dinosaur tail.

While we can't tell what dinosaur the tail could have been from, it's unmistakably from a dinosaur.

What's particularly fascinating is that it was from a feathered dinosaur, and the feathers have been immaculately preserved within the amber.

FACT 75

The Tyrannosaurus rex was named the "Tyrant King."

Quite literally, as that's what the name it was given translates to.

These fearsome beasties were some of the largest carnivorous dinosaurs, so it's easy to see where the name came from!

Despite being featured in Jurassic Park, they actually lived during the Cretaceous period.

FACT 76

The largest complete T-Rex skeleton ever discovered was named Sue.

Not the most terrifying name, we'll admit, but Sue the Tyrant King surely has a nice ring to it.

Sue was discovered by Sue Hendrickson and was later nicknamed in her honor.

She was certainly a massive creature, though, measuring 13 feet (4 m) tall at the hips and 40 feet (12.3 m) long.

FACT 77

More than fifty T-Rex skeletons have been unearthed.

Tyrannosaurus rexes have been found all over western North America, making them one of the more mobile dinosaurs of their time.

While many of the skeletons we've discovered were quite fragmented, quite a few of them were almost complete — hence why we have such great reconstructions of them!

FACT 78

The bite of a T-Rex had more force than any other creature that's ever walked on land.

According to recent calculations, they were capable of biting down on things with a force of 7.1 tons (6.5 tonnes) of force, about four times as much as a saltwater crocodile.

This type of force allowed them to bite straight through bone, and not just any bones, but giant dinosaur bones!

FACT 79

Colorado's official state dinosaur is the stegosaurus.

It was back in 1876 that the first stegosaurus fossil was discovered just outside of Denver, Colorado.

Named the "covered lizard," due to its protective scales, it was only officially designated as Colorado's state dinosaur in 1982.

100 Facts about Dinosaurs

FACT 80

Nicolas Cage once spent $276,000 on a rare dinosaur skull.

In 2007 Nicolas Cage outbid Leonardo Di Caprio for the skull of a Tyrannosaurus bataar, a close relative of the Tyrannosaurus rex.

Cage may have come to regret bidding so high, as, in 2014, it was discovered that the skull had previously been stolen from Mongolia.

Keen to do the right thing, Cage was quick to return the rare skull to the Mongolian government.

FACT 81

The Ankylosaurus magniventris had a huge club-like tail that it used to ward off predators.

While many herbivores were easy prey for predators like the Tyrannosaurus rex, the Ankylosaurus had the perfect defense.

Not only did it have a huge bony club at the end of its tail, but it also had spike-studded bony plates all over its body.

Its only weak spot was its soft underbelly, meaning predators would have to flip this defensive dinosaur onto its back – or find a weaker target!

FACT 82

The world's smallest dinosaur egg is smaller than a golf ball.

The 1.75 inches (45 mm) by 0.78 inches (20 mm) egg would have weighed just 0.35 ounces (10 g), about the same size and weight as a quail egg.

It's believed to be the egg of one of the theropods, two-legged carnivorous dinosaurs, and dates back to 110 million years ago.

FACT 83

The world's largest dinosaur eggs ever discovered were oviraptorosaur eggs.

Unearthed in the 1990s in China, these eggs measured about 1.6 feet (0.5 m) long!

While they were initially thought to have been Tyrannosaur eggs, when a fossilized embryo was discovered at the same site, it was realized they were from a huge species of oviraptorosaur.

FACT 84

The tallest known dinosaur reached heights up to 59 feet (18 m).

The sauroposeidon, whose name literally translates into "lizard earthquake god," couldn't have been named any better.

FACT 85

Stegosauruses and allosauruses often fought to the death.

For a long time, it was believed that the two often tussled, but there wasn't much evidence to go off.

Since the turn of the 21st century, a number of fossils have proved this theory, including one fossilized allosaur, which appears to have died from a wound caused by a stegosaurus' tail spike.

FACT 86

Many dinosaurs traveled in herds.

Dinosaurs were not unlike many modern animals as they were sociable creatures and tended to travel and live in large groups.

For herbivorous dinosaurs, this allowed greater protection from predators; for predators, this allowed greater success rates while hunting.

FACT 87

In Jurassic Park, the sounds used to create the T-Rex's roar were from an alligator, tiger & elephant.

Specifically, it was a combination of three recordings: a baby elephant's squeal, an alligator's gurgling, and an angry tiger's snarl.

The recordings were changed in speed to make them sound more menacing and realistic (we should really say "realistic," as we have no idea what they sounded like!).

FACT 88

It's likely that dinosaurs weren't cold-blooded.

While they likely weren't cold-blooded, like modern reptiles, they probably weren't warm-blooded either.

Instead, it's believed they found a middle ground between the two.

FACT 89

T-Rexes most likely only lived to a little over thirty years old.

From the fossils we've found so far, that is.

The oldest of which is nicknamed Trix was discovered in 2013 in Montana and is believed to be just over thirty years old.

The famous T-Rex, Sue, who we spoke of earlier, is estimated to have been about 28 years old.

FACT 90

Large sauropods likely had the longest lifespans out of all dinosaurs.

Dinosaurs such as the apatosaurus or diplodocus would have outlived all other dinosaurs, or so it seems.

While scientists initially believed they might have got as old as 300, that's now been scaled back to a meager 70-80 years – about the same age limit as elephants.

FACT 91

Sauropods likely ate more than 1 ton (907 kg) of plant matter daily.

Being the largest animals that ever walked the earth, it should be no surprise that their diets were equally enormous.

FACT 92

The largest plesiosaur was about 46 feet (14 m) long.

Imagine if you replaced a sauropod's chunky legs with sturdy flippers, shortened its tail a bit, gave it some vicious-looking teeth, and then threw it into the sea, and you've pretty much got a plesiosaurus on your hands.

This plesiosaur, specifically the Elasmosaurus platyurus, was both the longest and the heaviest plesiosaur, weighing approximately 24 tons (22 tonnes).

FACT 93

Triceratops was able to fight off tyrannosauruses with their massive horns.

The name Triceratops literally translates into "three-horned face," which is a little unimaginative if you ask me.

While probably helpful in attracting a potential mate, their horns were also likely used for defense.

One skeleton, for example, was found with a broken horn with tyrannosaurus bite marks on it.

FACT 94

Dilophosauruses didn't spit poison.

Jurassic Park got oh so many things wrong about this dinosaur.

It didn't spit poison, it didn't have a huge frill like a frill-necked lizard, and it wasn't even remotely that small!

To be fair, though, this double-crested dinosaur was still pretty awesome looking – it just wasn't quite as cool as the film made it out to be!

FACT 95

The smallest pterodactyl was about the size of a pigeon.

Nemicolopterus crypticus, discovered in northeastern China, would have flitted about from tree to tree chasing insects about 120 million years ago.

With a wingspan of just ten inches (25 cm), it's hard to imagine it could possibly have been related to the terrifying quetzalcoatlus!

FACT 96

Dinosaur bones that turned into opal have been found in Australia.

One of the most famous sets of opalized dinosaur fossils was a pair of dinosaur jawbone fragments, complete with teeth, that had a striking vein of opal running through the bone.

These pieces were later identified in 2017 to belong to an entirely new dinosaur species, Weewarrasaurus pobeni.

FACT 97

Fred Flintstones's pet dinosaur Dino was a snorkasaurus.

We're sad to say that a snorkasaurus is a completely fictional dinosaur, though.

That said, it's easy to see that the creation of Dino was definitely inspired by the sauropods, although Dino is significantly smaller.

FACT 98

If Godzilla was a real dinosaur, it would have been a type of theropod.

In 1998 a paleontologist attempted to figure out what type of dinosaur Godzilla might have been based on its anatomical features.

Ultimately, it was decided that Godzilla, at least the 90s version, would have been related to a group of theropods called ceratosaurs.

FACT 99

The time gap between when T-rexes & stegosauruses were alive is larger than the gap between humans & T-rexes.

Stegosauruses were around late in the Jurassic period, about 150 million years ago.

On the other hand, T-Rexes lived around 65 million years ago, during the Cretaceous period.

It really puts how long dinosaurs were around into scale when you think about it like this!

FACT 100

Some dinosaurs were absolutely massive, but none were bigger than blue whales.

Blue whales can weigh up to 190 tons (172.4 tonnes) and grow 110 feet (34 me) long. The largest dinosaurs weigh up to 69 tons (62.6 tonnes) and measure up to 120 feet (36.5 m) long.

In general, whales can grow much heavier as their weight is supported by water, while dinosaurs still had to support their weight with their legs!

Thank you!

Welcome to the world of **Tiki Taka**! If you've enjoyed this book, there's a treasure trove of other fascinating reads awaiting you. Dive into more engaging and entertaining books authored by me, filled with fun facts, quirky knowledge, and captivating insights. Explore a universe of learning and entertainment!

Milton Keynes UK
Ingram Content Group UK Ltd.
UKHW020415150324
439439UK00010B/1246